THE 1950s

Richard Tames

Franklin Watts
London · New York · Toronto · Sydney

© 1990 Franklin Watts

First published in Great Britain in 1990 by
Franklin Watts
96 Leonard Street
London EC2A 4RH

First published in the United States by
Franklin Watts Inc.
387 Park Avenue South
New York, N.Y. 10016

First published in Australia by
Franklin Watts Australia
14 Mars Road
Lane Cove
New South Wales 2066

UK ISBN: 0 86313 735 0

Design: K and Co
Editor: Hazel Poole
Picture Research: Jan Croot, Sarah Ridley
Printed in Belgium

A CIP catalogue record for
this book is available from
the British Library

Photographs: Associated Press 16(C), 17(B), 34(B); Norman Barrett 39(TL); British
Airways 41(TL); J. Allen Cash Photolibrary 25(CL); Cinerama 32(T); Jan Croot 28(R),
31(C), 31(B), 41(TR); Daily Mirror 7(BL), 15(B); Design Council 6(BL), 6(BR); Horace
Dobbs 21(TL); with gratitude to the EMI Music Archives 29(TR); with the kind
permission of Hertfordshire County Record Office 25(CL), 25(CR); Hulton-Deutsch
Collection 7(CR), 9(B), 12(B), 16(T), 19(BL), 19(BR), 22(BR), 23(B), 30(T), 30(BL),
31(TL), 33(T), 34(T), 35(TL), 36(T), 37(B), 39(TR), 39(BL), 41(C), 42(BR); Kobal
Collection 29(B), 30(BR), 32(B), 33(BL), 33(BR); Kontiki Museum, Oslo 21(TR);
Roger Mayne 35(B); Museum of London 23(T), 23(C); Novosti 19(TR); Popperfoto
7(T), 15(T), 15(C), 18(BL), 19(TL), 20(B), 21(B), 22(T), 22(BL), 26(BL), 27(TL),
27(TR), 27(C), 27(B), 29(C), 35(TR), 36(B), 37(TL), 37(TR), 38(T), 38(B), 40(T),
40(B), 41(B); Retrograph Archive Collection 28(BL); Science Photo Library 42(T),
43(T), 43(CL); Cecil Beaton photograph courtesy of Sotheby's London 26(BR); Tass
9(T); Topham 6(T), 7(CL), 8(T), 8(B), 9(C), 10(B), 11(TL), 11(TR), 11(B), 12(T),
13(T), 13(BL), 13(BR), 14(T), 14(B), 16(BR), 17(TL), 17(TR), 20(T), 39(BR), 42(BL),
43(B); UK Atomic Energy Authority 18(BR); Basil Spence Partnership/Mead Gallery,
Warwick University 25(TL); ZEFA 24(BL), 24(BR), 25(BL). (Map on p. 10 by Stan
Johnson).

cover: Popperfoto/Kobal Collection
frontispiece: Popperfoto

Contents

Introduction

The 1940s had seen most of the world's peoples gripped in the agony of war. The 1950s brought peace to most and a new prosperity to many. The United States emerged as the world's pre-eminent power, its forces scattered in military bases around the globe, its population enjoying a standard of living previously unknown to any nation in history and envied throughout the world. American prestige and self-confidence were blighted, however, by racial injustice and the fear of communism, both at home and abroad. Beside Soviet Russia arose a mighty new ally, a communist China, though their alliance was not to outlast the decade.

Britain hailed a new era with the coronation of a new Queen but, like France, struggled with colonial problems while their former enemies, Germany and Japan, astonished them with their vitality in rebuilding shattered economies. The creation of closer ties between the countries of western Europe promised well for the future but over all mankind was cast the shadow of the nuclear bomb.

In its impact on everyday life, however, the effect of ever-advancing technology was no less imposing. Television, cheap electrical appliances and mass-produced cars transformed the life-styles and leisure of millions, though these changes were largely confined to the western world. The peoples of Asia and Africa benefitted from more basic improvements in health and diet which helped to fuel a "population explosion" which was, in turn, to create new pressures for migration, urban growth and environmental damage. As the decade closed, the atomic age merged with the space age as satellite photographs showed more dramatically than ever before that today the world was one, however much its peoples were still divided and in conflict.

Britain in the 1950s

When Princess Anne was born in 1950 she was given a yellow identity card and a green ration book, entitling her to supplies of orange juice and cod liver oil. War-time controls were still in force, five years after the fighting had ended. But the baby Princess was also made the millionth member of the Automobile Association, a sign of the "affluence" that was to be the hallmark of the decade after twenty years of depression and rationing.

The Festival of Britain, marking the centenary of the Great Exhibition of 1851, proclaimed British vigour and inventiveness but the death of King George VI in 1952 brought a personal grief to millions. The accession of the young Queen was eagerly hailed as the opening of a new Elizabethan age. The death of Queen Mary (1867–1953) cut a last public link with the Victorian era, as did the running of London's last tram in 1952.

Politically, the emphasis was on continuity as successive Tory governments accepted the achievements of their Labour predecessors in creating a welfare state and publicly-controlled transport and utilities. It was not a time of bold new initiatives.

△ A London tram is forced to use headlights in fog at 10.30 a.m. "Clean air" laws which forced Londoners to burn "smokeless" fuels put an end to the legendary "Pea-soupers".

▷ The 27 acre site of the Festival of Britain on the South Bank of the River Thames was dominated by the futuristic-looking Skylon, an aluminium needle with no visible means of support – like Britain itself, some commented. The only permanent legacy of this celebration was the Royal Festival Hall, a long-overdue concert auditorium.

A "MODELCRAFT" MICROMODEL of THE SKYLON

FESTIVAL OF BRITAIN 1951

PRICE PURCHASE TAX·

▽ Harold Macmillan succeeded Eden as Prime Minister in 1957 and quickly restored close links with the United States. Waving a "premium bond", the new savings certificate which gave the buyer a monthly "flutter" in a computer-controlled sweep-stake, he told people "you've never had it so good"

SUPERMAC
HE'S TERRIFIC – HE'S STUPENDOUS – HE'S IRRESISTIBLE
SUPPORTED BY A CAST OF STRIKING "BLACKPOOL BELLES"
A SUPER · COLOSSAL · TOP · PRODUCTION IN TRUE·BLUE COLOUR
AND THE MONSTER FROM TRANSPORT HOUSE
CERT: U
TORYTZ
SUPERMAC
HOUSE FULL
12/6
"I TOLD YOU THIS SORT OF STUFF WILL FETCH 'EM BACK INTO THE OLD CINEMA..."

△ The coronation of Queen Elizabeth II (top) in June 1953 followed a 1,000 year old ritual – but television now let her subjects watch the event.

△ In April 1955, Sir Winston Churchill gave a dinner for the Queen at 10 Downing Street and announced his resignation as Prime Minister.

7

The communist world

By 1950, Russian-backed Communist parties had seized power throughout eastern Europe. The wartime "Grand Alliance" would be replaced by two armed camps – the North Atlantic Treaty Organisation (NATO) and the Russian-dominated Warsaw Pact. Distrust was fuelled by mutual espionage and rivalry in developing atomic weapons and spacecraft, but the violent confrontations of this "cold war" era took place outside divided Europe. In 1950, Korea, "temporarily" divided since 1945, saw the Communist government of the north try to reunify the country by force. The weak south turned to the United States for help. Aided by over a dozen allies, the United States, under a United Nations flag, finally stabilized the continued division of the country along the 38th parallel after three years of bloody fighting. Stalin's death in 1953 led to the secret trial and execution of his police chief, Beria, and the rise of Nikita Khrushchev as first secretary of the Communist Party. Khrushchev denounced Stalin's persecutions and proclaimed the hope of "peaceful co-existence" with the West but still crushed popular risings in Poland and Hungary. China, meanwhile, went its own way in adapting communism to its needs.

△ Bewildered civilians in Pyongyang, capital of North Korea, after its capture by American troops in October 1950. The Chinese took it back in December but lost it again in June 1951.

▽ Chinese troops crossing a river during their 1950 invasion of Tibet. A revolt in 1958 cost 65,000 Tibetan lives and forced the Dalai Lama, Tibet's spiritual leader, into exile in India.

◁ Muscovites read Pravda's black-bordered confirmation of Stalin's death in March 1953 after nearly thirty years of dictatorial rule. The full scale of his tyranny took another thirty years to be revealed.

▽ In November 1956, the Soviet Union sent tanks into Hungary to crush a national rising against its domination. 20,000 people died and 200,000 fled to the West as Russian control was re-asserted.

▽ In July 1959, Vice-President Richard M. Nixon, visiting Moscow, receives a playful gesture of peace from Soviet Premier Khrushchev at an American exhibition. In a mock-up of a gadget-filled American kitchen, the two then argued heatedly for an hour about the rival merits of capitalism and communism.

Europe

By the 1950s, the scars of war were healing in western Europe. Devastated West Germany made an "economic miracle" out of hard work, while Italy showed its old flair in films, fashion and design. Spain, still wretchedly poor, began to benefit from tourism. France, however, suffered from a succession of weak governments and colonial wars. Persistent efforts were made for closer co-operation, though ambitious plans for a "United States of Europe" failed. In 1951 Belgium, the Netherlands and Luxembourg (already joined as Benelux, a customs union) linked with France, Germany and Italy to form the European Coal and Steel Community, which formed the basis for the European Economic Community, set up by the Treaty of Rome in 1957. The Nordic Council of Scandinavian states was another example of practical co-operation.

European Free Trade Association

European Economic Community

Western Europe

▽ Signing the Allied-West German Peace Contract 1952. (Left to right) Eden, Schuman, Acheson and Adenauer.

▷ EFTA, the European Free Trade Association was set up in 1959 to rival the "Common Market".

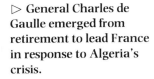

△ De Gaulle's 1958 landslide victory enabled him to begin the tricky task of French withdrawal from Algeria.

▷ General Charles de Gaulle emerged from retirement to lead France in response to Algeria's crisis.

▷ US garrison troops parade through the streets of Frankfurt in an "Army Day" march. In 1955 a partially re-armed West Germany was admitted to the NATO alliance but it was clear to most Germans that American forces were still needed to guarantee security against the Soviet threat.

Leaders rise and fall

Throughout Asia and Africa, the new politics of independence exacted a high price from its leaders. Assassins killed King Abdullah of Jordan and Prime Minister Liaquat Ali Khan of Pakistan in 1951, King Faisal of Iraq in 1958 and Prime Minister Bandaranaike of Sri Lanka in 1959. Luxury-loving King Farouk of Egypt was lucky to flee to comfortable exile after the 1952 army coup, as was Argentine dictator Juan Peron who unwisely threatened the authority of the Catholic Church.

But others showed remarkable staying power. Bourguiba of Tunisia achieved independence for his country in 1956 and was to stay its leader for thirty years. Lee Kuan Yew of Singapore was to do the same after becoming Prime Minister in 1959. Other major newcomers were Dr. Verwoerd, chief architect of South Africa's apartheid policies and visionary Kwame Nkrumah who led the wealthy Gold Coast to independence as Ghana in 1957, then drove it to near-bankruptcy. The best-loved world figure of the decade was undoubtedly Cardinal Roncalli who became Pope John XXIII in 1958.

△ The immense funeral cortege of Eva Peron in Buenos Aires. Ex-film star Evita used glamour and corruption to build her personal power.

▽ Hussein Ibn Talal leaves Amman's main mosque after being crowned King of Jordan on his 18th birthday. He is surrounded by Bedouin troops, on whose loyalty his rule depended. He survived many assassination attempts, pursuing a pro-Western policy and keeping close personal links with Britain's Royal family.

Scenting victory – Cypriot leader
Archbishop Makarios (top) is hailed
at Athens airport in 1959. Dr.
Hastings Banda (left) was imprisoned
by the British in 1959 but later led
Malawi to independence. Fidel
Castro (below) takes the oath of
office as Cuba's youngest ever Prime
Minister in 1959 after his guerrillas
overthrow dictator Batista.

Suez

In 1952, King Farouk of Egypt was overthrown by a "Free Officers" movement in the army. They wanted to end ties with Britain, who regarded control of the Suez Canal as vital for the defence of her world-wide empire and trade. In 1954, an Anglo-Egyptian treaty withdrew British troops from the Canal Zone but the British and French governments kept control of the Suez Canal Company which ran the international waterway. When western powers refused to aid Egypt in building its Aswan Dam project, Free Officers' leader Colonel Nasser took over the Canal Company in July 1956 to use its profits to pay for the Dam. Both sides saw the issue as a matter of national pride and repeated negotiations failed to find a compromise on the future of the canal. Britain and France prepared for war, secretly agreeing that Israel should attack Egypt, so that they could claim to be separating the two sides in the interests of peaceful users of the canal. On 29 October, Israel invaded the Sinai peninsula. An Anglo-French invasion on 5 November was called off under pressure from the United States. Nasser's success led Syria to join Egypt to form the United Arab Republic.

▷ Israeli troops gather to attack Egyptian outposts in Sinai. The peninsula was to remain in Israeli hands until a negotiated withdrawal in 1982.

◁ All smiles in 1955 as Eden, Britain's Foreign Secretary, visits Cairo. But Eden privately considered Nasser a dictator to be met by force if necessary.

(Below opposite) Crowds in Alexandria applaud Nasser's announcement of the Suez Canal take-over. The failed Anglo-French invasion made him a hero.

△ Troops of a United Nations emergency peace-keeping force arrive as British paratroopers depart. The United Nations provided a forum for international denunciation of Britain and France.

ISRAEL'S SHIPS BARRED BY EGYPT FOR 7 YEARS

Vicky

"THE CANAL MUST BE RUN EFFICIENTLY AND KEPT OPEN, AS IT HAS ALWAYS BEEN IN THE PAST, AS A FREE AND INTERNATIONAL WATERWAY FOR THE SHIPS OF ALL NATIONS"

◁ British cartoonist Vicky satirises Eden as a latter-day Admiral Nelson, deliberately ignoring obvious dangers to pursue his own plans. Unlike Nelson, Eden found that stubbornness and misjudgment were to cost him his career. He resigned as Prime Minister in January 1957.

15

Ending empires

The former greatness of the European powers rested in part on their possession of overseas empires. Whatever their economic value, which was often questionable, they conferred political prestige and diplomatic leverage. Exhausted as a result of World War II, however, Europe increasingly lacked both the will and the means to resist colonial demands for the rights that Europeans themselves enjoyed in terms of self-government.

Both the French and the Dutch fought vainly to reassert their power by force. Britain finally accepted the inevitable once it had decided to part with India in 1947. In Malaya, however, British troops fought skilfully and successfully to defeat a Communist rebellion before handing over power in 1957.

△ "Mau Mau" suspects in a Kenyan prison camp. This rural rebellion, part tribal war, part conflict for land, cost 235 European and 13,000 African lives between 1952 and 1960.

△ In April 1955 representatives of 29 African and Asian states met at Bandung in Indonesia in an attempt to distance themselves from the "cold war" confrontations of the super-powers.

▷ The Duchess of Kent dances with Kwame Nkrumah at a ball to mark Ghanaian independence – a symbol of British willingness to end colonial rule without prolonged bloodshed.

◁ Tunisia's Habib Bourguiba (1903–) managed to achieve a peaceful disengagement from French rule in 1956 but kept his country on economically beneficial terms with the former imperial power.

△ French paratroopers counter-attacking a Viet Minh site. The long French effort to reassert control over Indo-China ended in defeat at Dien Bien Phu, a French trap in which the French were themselves entrapped.

◁ The struggle for Algerian independence from France led to terror and torture on both sides. Here French troops round up suspected "rebel sympathisers". The French army remained unbeaten but the war so divided France that it lost the will to hold on.

The atomic age

In 1950 the United States began research to make a "super bomb", more powerful than the one that had wiped out Hiroshima in 1945. In November 1952 an experimental "device" vapourized Eniwetok Atoll in the Marshall Islands of the Pacific into a mushroom cloud of dust 25 miles (40 kilometres) high and 100 miles (161 kilometres) across and in 1953, Russia tested an actual bomb. By 1955, both Russia and the United States were already at least willing to talk about nuclear disarmament as eminent scientists issued the "Pugwash manifesto", calling for a halt to the atomic arms race. By 1957 Britain, too, had its own "H-bomb". That year Britain's 'White Paper on Defence' admitted "... There is at present no means of providing adequate protection for the people of this country against nuclear attack". The most people could hope for was a four minute warning of the approach of missiles. In 1958, Nobel prize-winner Linus Pauling presented the United Nations with the signatures of 9,000 scientists, stressing the genetic danger from even testing nuclear weapons and calling for their ending. This was supported by mass protests in both the United States and Britain. But the cost of the arms race was probably more decisive in leading to the 1963 partial "test ban treaty", long after both sides had stockpiled enough bombs to achieve Mutually Assured Destruction – MAD.

◁ Troops of the 11th US Airborne Division watch an A-bomb test outside Las Vegas, Nevada as part of a combined manoeuvres exercise. As time passed, it became clear that even such limited exposure could drastically increase the risks of developing cancer.

▽ Queen Elizabeth II opening Britain's first atomic power station at Calder Hall in 1956. In 1955 the government announced its plans to build 12 nuclear plants over the next 10 years.

◁ The Campaign for Nuclear Disarmament (CND), set up in 1958 with philosopher Bertrand Russell as its president, organised what became an annual march between the atomic research centre at Aldermaston and a rally in Trafalgar Square.

△ The Soviet Union's nuclear-powered ice-breaker *Lenin* showed the practical uses of the atom. In 1957 the US nuclear submarine, *Nautilus*, sailed under the North Pole, opening a new dimension in secret warfare.

▷ In February 1950, Dr. Klaus Fuchs, a German-born Communist working in British atomic research was charged with giving secret data to the Soviet Union following an FBI tip-off. He may have saved the Soviets an estimated ten years of research and this fear hastened the western commitment to make an "H-bomb" to keep ahead of Russia. Sentenced to 14 years in prison and deprived of his British citizenship, Fuchs was freed in 1959 and deported to East Germany. Fuchs's interrogation led eventually to the denunciation of Ethel and Julius Rosenberg as atom spies in the United States. They were sentenced to death. Protesting their innocence, they went to the electric chair in June 1953.

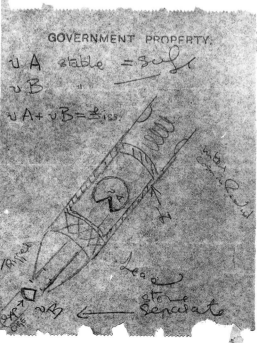

Exploration and adventure

By the mid-twentieth century, few regions of the world's surface remained undiscovered but the challenge to penetrate its heights and depths remained and increasingly relied on advances in science and technology. The conquest of Everest, for example, depended on the meticulous observation of weather conditions by expedition leader John Hunt and the use of such hi-tech novelties as high altitude nylon clothing and light-weight oxygen equipment.

Exploration was becoming essentially a team effort and one determined as much by the funds and initiatives of government as by the courage and daring of individuals. 1958 saw both American and New Zealand scientific teams at the South Pole, while a British expedition under Dr. Vivian Fuchs made the first overland crossing of the Antarctic.

In 1959, a further hopeful sign for the future was a twelve nation agreement on a draft treaty to keep the whole Antarctic region as a demilitarized scientific reserve, open to all nations and free from pressures for commercial development. And if science and the systematic approach threatened to take the romance out of exploration, film and television now enabled distant millions to see it happen before their own eyes.

△ New Zealander Edmund Hillary photographed by Nepali sherpa Tenzing Norgay at the summit of Mount Everest, 29,002 feet above sea-level, on 29 May 1953. News of their triumph reached Britain on the morning of Queen Elizabeth II's coronation.

◁ An ice-pick marks the relative size of the alleged "footprint" of a yeti. This 1951 photo was followed by unconfirmed sightings of the Himalayas' legendary "Abominable Snowman" by later expeditions.

△ Norwegian Thor Heyerdahl's "Kontiki" expedition saw a five man crew sail a balsa wood raft 5,000 miles (6,400 kilometres) to show that Polynesians might have come from South America originally by sea.

△ Diver wearing an aqualung, invented by the French explorer Commander Jacques Cousteau. He developed underwater television techniques from his ship *Calypso* to reveal the underwater world of sea-bed life in his 1956 film *The Silent World.*

▷ *USS Glacier* ploughs through the Ross Sea as part of "Operation Deep Freeze", a co-operative American – New Zealand scientific investigation of conditions in the Antarctic.

Uncovering the past

1952 was an epoch-making year for the understanding of the remote past. Young Michael Ventris cracked the secret of 'Linear B', the ancient script which had puzzled generations of scholars, and in the same year the invention of radio-carbon dating gave archaeologists a revolutionary new method of accurately estimating the age of once-living materials, like wood or cloth, for as far back as 4,500 years. The year closed with the discovery by scientists in South Africa of the coelacanth, a species of fish thought to have been extinct for over 40,000,000 years.

Archaeology continued to grab the headlines throughout the decade. In 1953, W. Le Gros Clark demonstrated conclusively that the so-called 'Piltdown Man' – 'Eoanthropus dawsonii' – was nothing but an elaborate hoax that had fooled the experts for over forty years by combining a human skull and an ape jaw to produce a 'missing link' in the evolutionary chain. Important excavations of the 1950s dealt with Nonsuch Palace, Elizabeth I's favoured retreat, and the 'Vasa', a remarkably preserved 17th century Swedish warship.

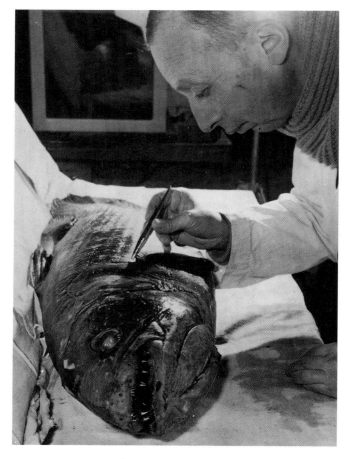

△ Examining one of three coelacanth caught off Madagascar.

◁ The head of 'Tollund man' found, preserved by mud, in Denmark in 1956.

▽ Mr. Alvan Marston had long held the notion of 'Piltdown man' to be an error but argued that previous experts had made a genuine mistake and not fallen for a hoax.

△ 1954 saw the unearthing near the official residence of London's Lord Mayor, of a temple to Mithras, a god of courage much worshipped by Roman soldiers. The bull was a sacrificial animal, whose blood symbolized renewal of life.

◁ Michael Ventris deciphering 'Linear B'. The young British scholar recognised the script as an early form of Greek and was able to translate thousands of clay tablets from the Mycenaean period (1400–1000 BC) of Bronze Age Greece.

Building for the future

In the western world, war prevented major building projects in the early 1940s. The main task was the reconstruction of basic facilities. The 1950s saw a renewal of interest in more ambitious schemes. The high priest of modern design was Charles-Édouard Jeanneret better known as 'Le Corbusier'. His followers applauded his buildings as clean, simple and uncluttered. Critics called them cold, impossible to live in, even ugly.

In their view his 'international' style was simply filling the skyline of the world's great cities with filing cabinets. As if to reassert their own established reputations the leading architects of the previous generation produced outstanding new buildings – Mies van der Rohe's Seagram Building and Frank Lloyd Wright's Guggenheim Museum.

But many people had more basic worries. A 1950 survey showed that nearly half of all British homes still had no bathroom. A major government initiative was to announce the building of 'New Towns', some in a ring around London, to decant bombed-out residents, others in decayed industrial areas. All were to have low density housing, separation of traffic and pedestrians and a mix of social classes.

Plans were also announced for a new Underground Line and a Channel Tunnel – which took 30 years to happen.

◁ Brasilia – Brazil's new capital in the interior. The futuristic buildings and bold bow-and-arrow plan suggested a nation's self-confident thrust towards greatness.

△ The headquarters of the United Nations opened in 1951. In theory designed by a committee, it was based on the inspiration of one member – Le Corbusier.

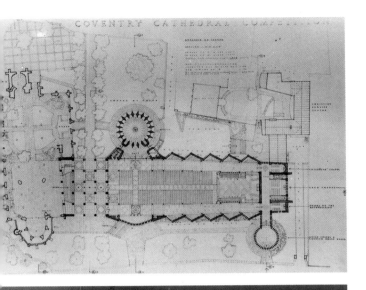

◁ Coventry Cathedral – a symbol of Britain's post-war recovery, blending old and new. Sir Basil Spence's competition designs, submitted in 1951, incorporated the shell of its bombed-out Gothic predecessor.

▽ Hatfield New Town in Hertfordshire. Like Crawley, Basildon and Harlow it was intended to take London's "overspill" population. New residents found the large open green spaces often bleak and inconvenient.

◁ Le Corbusier's most famous saying – "A house is a machine for living in" put him firmly in the camp of the 'functionalists'. His own designs – the chapel at Ronchamp, the Indian city of Chandigarh, large-scale housing at Marseilles – in the long run mattered less than his enormous influence on the professions of architecture and planning.

Art and design

According to Sir Hugh Casson, design mastermind of the "Festival of Britain", the chaotic "taste" of the 1950s was an understandable reaction against the drab 1940s – "After ten years of austerity . . . people wanted the sensation of plenty . . . The result was . . . a binge of far too many colours and textures and changes of surface . . . It was like going into a sweet shop after being on a starvation diet."

In the visual arts, similar confusion seemed to reign on both sides of the Atlantic, with a widening gulf between the professional artist and the ordinary public. Britain's world-class sculptors Barbara Moore and Eduardo Paolozzi were enthused over by the artistic establishment but ridiculed by the popular press. When it came to painting there was widespread acclaim for Pietro Annigoni's romantic portrait of the Queen but disquiet and disgust at the disturbingly nightmarish visions of Francis Bacon.

▽ Cecil Beaton's photographic model with a creation of "action painter" Jackson Pollock, who said "When I am painting I have no knowledge of what I am doing". Most people believed him.

△ British Sculptor Henry Moore with a terra cotta "Seated Figure" bearing an unusually striking resemblance to what one might expect such a subject to be.

△ Graham Sutherland's portrait of Churchill, commissioned by Parliament to mark the great man's 80th birthday was dismissed by its subject as 'a remarkable work of modern art' and later destroyed on his orders.

(Top right) The 'Ideal Home' of the 1950s favoured the open plan concept, doing away with internal walls where possible to create a sense of greater space and light.

(Centre right) Wallpapers, carpets and curtains with bold geometric designs in primary colours were seen as a revolt against the drab 'utility' patterns of war.

▷ Furniture of the 1950s favoured spindly legs and plastic or 'textured' coverings. The brand names Ercol and G-Plan became synonymous with modern decor.

Popular music

The 1950s saw popular music begin its transition into 'pop'. In 1950 the crooner, backed by a big band, and the lavishly costumed stage musical, still reigned supreme. By the end of the decade, however, they had lost their young audiences to their new rivals – rock'n' roll, "trad" jazz and, in Britain, skiffle, a sort of do-it-yourself country music played on home-made instruments, like the washboard and tea-chest double bass.

In 1950, Frank Sinatra was seen to replace Bing Crosby as America's highest-paid singer. "You can hear every word he sings – which is sometimes a pity" – remarked one critic but his London debut was still a sell-out. 1951 saw success on both sides of the Atlantic for *Kiss Me Kate* and *South Pacific*.

The decade closed with the death of jazz singer Billie Holiday at the age of 44. The development of higher quality recording techniques ('hi-fi') would ensure that generations yet unborn would be able to recapture the magic of her voice.

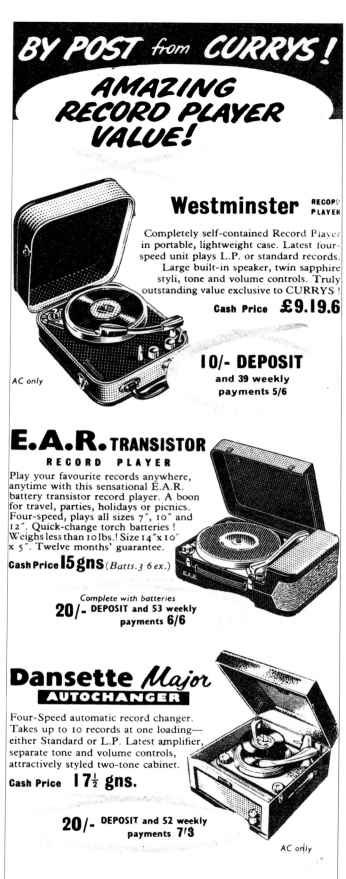

PEOPLE WILL SAY WE'RE IN LOVE

The THEATRE GUILD *presents at* The THEATRE ROYAL, *Drury Lane.*

OKLAHOMA!

(Based on the play GREEN GROW THE LILACS *by Lynn Riggs)*

Music by RICHARD RODGERS
Book and Lyrics by OSCAR HAMMERSTEIN 2ND

SONGS FROM THE SHOW
PEOPLE WILL SAY WE'RE IN LOVE ● THE SURREY WITH THE FRINGE ON TOP
OUT OF MY DREAMS ● OH, WHAT A BEAUTIFUL MORNIN'
I CAIN'T SAY NO ● OKLAHOMA
PRICE 2/- EACH, NET

WILLIAMSON MUSIC INC., NEW YORK

◁ Songs from American musicals like *Oklahoma, South Pacific* and *Carousel* became "standards", appealing to all ages.

△ Lightweight record players could transform a school hall into a dance hall or bring the stars to your own room.

▷ The slowly-revolving ($33\frac{1}{3}$ revolutions per minute) "long player", pressed in lightweight vinyl, offered an average of 20–25 minutes uninterrupted music per side – six tunes or a couple of movements of a symphony. Stacked ten high on a record-player this meant music for an entire evening. The LP's reign was to last for over thirty years until it was displaced by the even more portable cassette and compact disc.

△ Frank Sinatra being politely mobbed in London. Even the police look happy. Adoration of later American imports looked much more alarming to the older generation.

▷ *The Boyfriend* by Sandy Wilson – a 1953 musical set in the 1920s, was staged in England to huge success. The 29-year-old composer spent the rest of his career re-staging it worldwide.

Rock and roll

One, two, three o'clock, four o'clock rock!
Five, six, seven o'clock, eight o'clock rock!
Nine, ten, eleven o'clock, twelve o'clock rock!
We're gonna rock around the clock tonight
Rock, rock, rock till broad daylight
We're gonna rock, rock, rock around the clock,
tonight!

The film was *Blackboard Jungle* and the band was Bill Haley and the Comets. In 1955, *Rock Around the Clock* stayed at the top of the charts for five months. In 1956 it became the title of a film about the new dance and music craze – rock 'n' roll. Britain's own stars, had names hinting at impatience and violence – Marty Wilde, Billy Fury and Vince Eager. America kept in the headlines when three stars – Buddy Holly, Richie Valens and "Big Bopper", J. P. Richardson, died in a plane crash in 1959. For many, rock 'n' roll was a way of saying goodbye to childhood and 'No' to being grown-up.

△ Johnny Ray serenades fans under his dressing-room window in Dublin. Like Sinatra, he had the knack of singing close to the microphone as though the only people present were him and each single member of the audience. His appeal was heightened by his well-publicised deafness.

△ Bill Haley and the Comets traded ballads for beat and sold 22,000,000 records in two years before new stars made them look old and old-fashioned.

▷ Cliff Richard in *Espresso Bongo*, a film satirising the rise of a talentless pop star. The grand old man of British pop was still having the last laugh 30 years later.

◁ Tommy Steele (once Tommy Hicks) impresses young fans at his family home in south London's Bermondsey.

◁ Elvis Presley made a record for his mother's birthday in 1953. Three years later he was on TV at $50,000 a time and seeing his first hit record, *Heartbreak Hotel*, sell 3,000,000 copies. In the next two years he earned $100,000,000. In 1958 he began two years military service as a GI in Germany.

▽ The great thing about rock 'n' roll dancing was that there were no set steps to learn. As Bill Haley said, "Its appeal is its simplicity. Everyone wants to get into the act. With rock 'n' roll they can join in".

PICTUREGOER December 28 1957

12

WHY YOU'... G A BAD NAME

BY ... ...S BY ALLEN NEWTON

Seventeen-year-old Beryl Green is just one of the youngsters who can't resist that music

Take the ex... and I had at Britain's ...

Getting on for a thous... over the chalet terraces that sur... giant BUTLINS neon sign at Clacton, Essex. It was, in its way, an experiment. And I believe we . . . it showed just how easy it is for you pop fans to get a bad name.

It all depends on whether little groups of hotheads, devil-bent on stirring trouble, are persuasive enough to get the majority on their side. Usually, honours go to the level-headed majority; sometimes the hotheads get *their* way. That's when the headlines sizzle.

Just once during the festival weekend big trouble seemed to be brewing. The bandsmen had packed up, the Viennese ballroom had emptied. Rumour insisted that an all-night rock 'n roll session to records was to start in the smaller Regency hall.

A couple of hundred cats turned up. "Sorry," announced officials, "it was just a rumour. Let's

...e of the young men ...idn't like that. They ..., ripped them, threw

... and "Carve up" ...e dozen or so lads in ... Not many others took ... was enough to make ... grab the microphone. ... half pleading.
... what gave modern music ... as what the press wanted ...at would appear in head-
... riots . . . as he spoke a ... lit the dimmed hall for a ... that picture," hissed a ...ameraman," and the boys'll ...ou."
... listened as the situation be- ... One of the group walked over ... d grumbled to a little cluster ... "Treating us like kids . . . ... go to bed.

...urnalists, a reporter from a daily, ... "You've paid your money," he ...nough. Why shouldn't you have ...ession?"
A mag... photographer whispered to me: "Not much happening really . . . suppose I nip out and call the police . . . it'll make a picture."

A few of the thwarted rock 'n roll boys formed their own impromptu band, played a few numbers, then gave up. Most of the youngsters were drifting off chalet-wards, to bed or to all-night parties that left the lawns littered with beer bottles and cigarette stubs.

At one party couples jived around a bit, then pepped up the steps for a couple of photographers. A young man grabbed a beer bottle, bashed it against a wall and waved around the evilly jagged weapon.

He didn't move; just lolled against the wall. If he'd taken one step he'd have fallen flat on his face. No one took any notice of him. He put the broken bottle down, leaned there, just brooding.

Four lads on the lawn tilted beer bottles to

their lips; they looked a bit young to be guzzling that way. A girl sat in a wicker chair, a young man kneeling at her feet; his arms were round her waist. He kissed her, she kissed him. There were a few slightly ribald jeers.

Does all this sound evil, depraved, degenerate? Of course not. Misguided in some cases, maybe. Prey to misrepresentation, too easy to exaggerate . . . yes indeed. And that's the trouble.

I've *seen* reporters too eager to get a story, photographers too anxious to get a picture. I've *watched* a few trouble-makers, a few frustrated exhibitionists try to whip up the sort of frenzy in which they glory. I've *heard* the few try to incite the many.

The pity of it is; the many have to share the blame. Some of the youngsters I spoke to at Clacton admitted that their mums and dads weren't happy about it all, or at best couldn't understand why decent young people wanted to get mixed up in it.

Valerie Madre, for instance. She's eighteen, lives at Langley, in Buckinghamshire, works as a secretary in an important West End theatrical agency. She's blonde, very attractive, speaks well.

"Daddy used to be a jazz fan," she told me, "but now he disapproves of THIS. He says it's only for Teddy Boys."

She looked around, couldn't see a Teddy Boy anywhere. Her friend Maureen Sansom, twenty-one, a Soho clerk, said her folks "never seemed to have heard of these things."

Four teenage girls from Felixstowe—"nothing ever happens there"—admitted that their parents were a bit scared by the stories of rock 'n roll riots, had given strict instructions that the girls should stay clear of them.

The parents needn't have worried. The girls enjoyed themselves quite amply on the dance floor. And that's the point: pop music fans, rock 'n rollers, the cats . . . they're just high-spirited, energetic youngsters who can't resist that music beat.

SO A FEW HOTHEADS ACT LIKE STUPID, DAZED OR CRAZED ADOLESCENTS. WHY GIVE ALL THE YOUNGSTERS A BAD NAME BECAUSE OF THIS?

Pam Bilshaw comes from Felixstowe. There's much more fun at the festival than in the old home town

Some of the youngsters showed their harmless high spirits by having an all-night party on the lawns after the dancing

...others wanted an impromptu rock 'n roll session. For a moment the situation looked edgy, but it all ended quietly

Even a jazz festival must end. So it's "Knees Up, Mother Brown" at the station before catching the train back home

Joe Harriott blows hot as the Tony Kinsey Quintet... there was real quality music at the Clacton...

Film and theatre

In the 1950s most people still thought of films in terms of Hollywood and stars and as a form of entertainment. Intellectuals, who saw films as "art", raved about directors – from France (Tati, Truffaut), Italy (Fellini, de Sica), Sweden (Bergman) and even India (Satyajit Ray). Both types of film-goer, however, were gripped by the cult surrounding the magnetic James Dean, who only made three films before being killed in a car crash at the age of 24. The theatre remained mainly British and, despite the provocations of so-called *Angry Young Men*, relied on a diet of traditional classics and safe conventional dramas by Terence Rattigan, while nurturing fine young talents like actors Richard Burton and Kenneth More and directors Peter Hall and Joan Littlewood. In 1959, the City of London opened its first new theatre for three hundred years – the Mermaid, brainchild of actor/director Bernard Miles. Opera fans meanwhile thrilled to the arrival of a stunning Greek soprano, Maria Callas and ballet fans took a justifiable pride in the rise to fame of a home-grown talent, Margot Fonteyn.

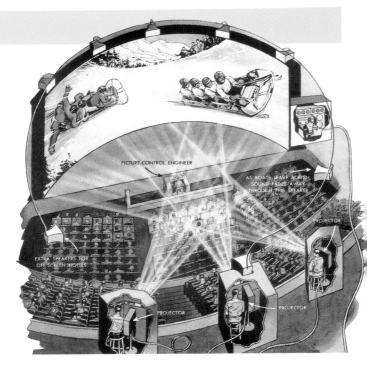

△ In 1952, Cinerama, used combat-simulation technology for pilots to produce a "wide-screen" effect, overwhelming audiences with the sense of "being there".

▽ Hollywood reclaimed its old superiority in the 1950's with lavish epics like *Ben Hur.* This film spectacular, starring Charlton Heston, was released in 1959.

◁ *Look Back in Anger* by John Osborne, was first produced at the Royal Court Theatre. Its hero, university drop-out Jimmy Porter, stood for the confused discontentment of 1950s British youth, rejecting a decayed imperial past and frustrated by snobbery and emotional narrowness. Newspapers identified an "Angry Young Man" school of writers which included Kingsley Amis, Alan Sillitoe and John Braine.

▽ *A Streetcar Named Desire* (1951) not only launched Marlon Brando as a star name but also established his "scratch and mumble" style of super-realistic acting as the model for later youth heroes such as James Dean and Paul Newman.

▽ *Some Like It Hot*, starring Marilyn Monroe and Jack Lemmon, was a slick comedy classic that long out-lasted the decade in popular appeal. By 1957 "MM" was married to playwright Arthur Miller and playing opposite Laurence Olivier.

Growing up

The war years of the 1940s brought home to every nation the obvious truth that its children were its future. In Britain, concentrated orange juice was provided by the government for infants. Child-rearing became a serious business. *Baby and Child Care* by Dr. Benjamin Spock, published in the United States in 1946 and in Britain in 1955, sold over 20,000,000 copies. *The Eagle*, a weekly colour comic, edited by a vicar, was launched in 1950 to provide British children with a healthy alternative to ghoul-packed American 'horror comics'.

BBC radio began *Listen with Mother* in 1951 with the immortal words 'Are you sitting comfortably?... Then we'll begin'. Young listeners remained loyal to *Uncle Mac* and *Children's Hour*, while older ones chuckled at the *Goons*, the first comedians to invent a style of humour specially for radio. American children could enjoy a more direct encounter with fantasy when the first Disneyland opened in California in 1955.

△ The 1950s were filled with new experiences that were a by-product of changing lifestyles. Rising car-ownership, for example, made people better-travelled than ever before.

▷ Teddy Boys were the aggressive face of youth, though their threat to public order was exaggerated by the press. But some *did* carry flick-knives and bicycle-chains.

◁ The hula-hoop was so called because it needed a gyration of the hips like a Hawaiian hula dancer to keep it going. Promoted as fun for all ages it was funniest for manufacturers who made them for pence to sell for pounds.

◁ Coffee bars, selling
frothy 'espresso' in
modern surroundings
were the teenage equiv-
alent of the adults' pub.

△ "Hand jive" gave
youngsters a way to join
in with music where it
was too crowded to
dance.

Fashion

Generally speaking only two social groups cared much about fashion in the 1950s – the well-off, who were the traditional market for Paris-based designers, and the working young generation, a new and rapidly-growing mass-market for High Street chain stores. Middle class girls still dressed to look like their mothers, who dressed as though they were still in the 1930s, wearing hats, gloves and pearls on every conceivable occasion.

Young working people, however, looked to America, mirrored through the cinema and magazines, for their inspiration and imported blue jeans, check shirts, sloppy sweaters and suede shoes. In 1955 Mary Quant opened 'Bazaar' in the King's Road, Chelsea to sell simple clothes in casual styles. Henceforth fashion history would run in reverse with the old and rich imitating their younger social inferiors.

△ 'Teddy Boys' got their name from the echo of the Edwardian era suggested by their flamboyant dress. In fact the American river-boat gambler, with his 'string' tie, draped jacket and gaudy waistcoat was a more likely model.

◁ In the 1950s Americans rediscovered jeans, the tough blue denim work-trousers originally invented for the western cow-hand. The craze reached Britain in 1955, but were seen at first as only a woman's garment.

△ The simple floral print cotton summer dress retained its popularity throughout the 1950s, despite the occasional efforts of British fashion manufacturers to imitate the more extreme styles of Parisian haute couture.

△ For younger women cheap, bright cottons were widely popular for the summer. Comfortable to wear and simple in design they suggested an active and care-free way of life.

▷ Only working-class young men were drawn to the eye-catching Teddy Boy style. Other males remained traditional and wore hats to cover slicked-back hair. The cut-down duffle coat hints at memories of wartime service in the navy.

Sport

Better communications, both through jet flights and the spread of television, gave sport an increasingly international character throughout the decade. The 1952 (Helsinki) and 1956 (Melbourne) Olympics provided grand set-piece contests. In Helsinki, Czech Emil Zatopek won the 10,000 metres and 5,000 metres and then entered his first ever marathon to win that as well. In Melbourne, Australia's women swimmers and athletes stole the show.

There were other shocks, too. In 1950, England entered soccer's World Cup for the first time only to be knocked out 1–0 by an amateur American side. England returned the compliment in 1951 when the unknown Randolph Turpin defeated Sugar Ray Robinson for the middleweight world title. Record-breakers of the decade included American Florence Chadwick, who in 1950 swam the English Channel in 13 hours 23 minutes; jockey Lester Piggott, who won the Derby, England's premier flat race, at the age of 18 in 1954; Donald Campbell, who set a new world water-speed record of 202 mph in 1955; and 21 year old Garfield Sobers of the West Indies who set a new record Test cricket score in 1958, hammering 365 off Pakistan – not out. In the same year, Australian Herb Elliott set new world records in both the mile and 1500 metres.

△ On May 6, 1954 Roger Bannister became the first man to run a mile in under four minutes.

◁ Betty Cuthbert, star of the Australian team, winning the 100 metres in Melbourne. She won the 200 metres as well.

(Far left) In November 1953, Hungary defeated England 6–3. The visitors' superior skills brought a new respect for "continental" style soccer with its emphasis on ball skills rather than physical contact.

Forward Bobby Charlton was one of the lucky survivors of the tragic Munich air crash in 1958 which killed seven of his Manchester United team mates.

(Below left) In 1951 Maureen "Little Mo" Connolly became, at 16, the youngest ever winner of the US Tennis championships.

▽ In 1951, Rocky Marciano (right) – world heavyweight champion (1952–56) – knocked former champion Joe Louis out of the ring.

On the move

The spread of motor car ownership in the 1950s was promoted by the desire of manufacturers to use mass-production techniques to bring motoring within the reach of the largest possible number. America pioneered not only in this but in creating a whole new lifestyle which revolved around having a car. The number of drive-in cinemas in the United States, for example, doubled to 2,200 in the single year of 1950. Britain lagged behind until the end of petrol rationing in 1950 and the onset of a motor manufacturer's 'price-war' in 1953. Major steps forward came in 1959 with the unveiling of Sir Alec Issigonis' revolutionary new 'Mini' car and the opening of a stretch of the M1. By that time Londoners had become familiar with yet another American import – the parking meter. In the air, Britain challenged more successfully. In 1951, a Canberra jet bomber set a new 4 hours 40 minutes record for crossing the Atlantic and 1958 saw BOAC introduce the world's first scheduled transatlantic air service. The 'Flying Bedstead', a 1954 experiment in vertical take-off, and the 'hovercraft' also promised well for the future.

△ In 1959, Britain's *Flying Saucer*, the Saunders Roe 'Hovercraft', made history on the 50th anniversary of Louis Bleriot's flight across the Channel by crossing from Calais to Dover in 2 hours 3 minutes on its 10 inch cushion of air. Bleriot had done it in 43 minutes.

◁ A drive-in cinema at Barajas, outside Madrid. Unpredictable weather conditions in Europe, and the lower average level of car-ownership, meant that the drive-in remained largely an American phenomenon.

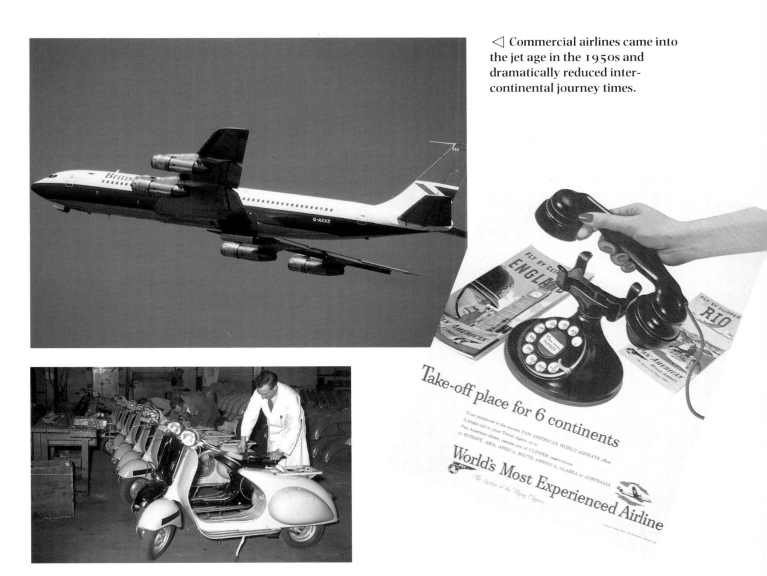

◁ Commercial airlines came into the jet age in the 1950s and dramatically reduced inter-continental journey times.

△ Nippy Vespa and Lambretta motor scooters from Italy offered a new rival to the traditional motorbike. Their sleek styling was attractive and hire-purchase payment schemes put them within reach of the teenager.

▷ The Ford Anglia, a cheap two-door family saloon, ideal for the weekend motorist. The box-like shape of the late 1950s replaced more rounded flowing lines to become standard in the 1960s.

Science and medicine

The launching of the Russian satellite *Sputnik* in October 1957 stunned the United States and marked the beginning of a "space race" between the superpowers. A month later, "space dog" Laika became the first living creature to orbit the earth. In 1958, American Explorer satellites revealed for the first time the existence of belts of radiation around the earth. They were named in honour of James Van Allen, their discoverer. Medicine saw numerous "firsts" in the course of the decade – kidney transplant, artificial hearts used in surgery, inserted heart pacemakers, an oral contraceptive pill and sex-change operations. Less happily it also saw the first widespread use of the drug Thalidomide which was to deform thousands of babies. Practical technological advances included direct telephone dialling, xerox machines, fan heaters, non-stick pans, new artificial textiles Orlon and Terylene, transistor radios and fish fingers.

▷ In March 1953, Dr. Jonas E. Salk announced success in tests of his new vaccine against the child killer-disease, polio – 'infantile paralysis'. In 1954, in the first mass-vaccination 1,829,916 Michigan children were immunized.

◁ In April 1953, Crick and Watson announced their analysis of the "double helix" structure of deoxyribonucleic acid (DNA) – the genetic material which governs the basic process of reproduction.

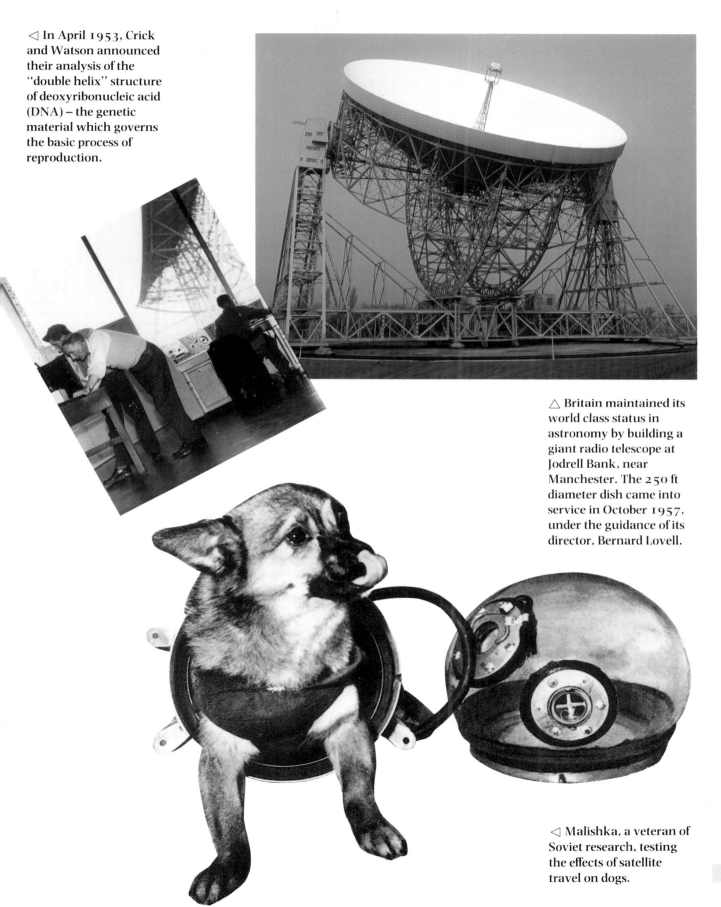

△ Britain maintained its world class status in astronomy by building a giant radio telescope at Jodrell Bank, near Manchester. The 250 ft diameter dish came into service in October 1957, under the guidance of its director, Bernard Lovell.

◁ Malishka, a veteran of Soviet research, testing the effects of satellite travel on dogs.

Personalities of the 1950s

Adenauer, Konrad (1876–1967), former mayor of Cologne who became the first Chancellor of the Federal Republic of Germany (1949–63).

Bernstein, Leonard (1918–), American conductor who composed the music for *West Side Story* (1957).

Bevan, Aneurin (1897–1960), British Labour politician and creator of the National Health Service, renowned for his public speaking and biting wit.

Bevin, Ernest (1881–1951), British Foreign Secretary and architect of NATO, "the dreadnought of the Labour Party".

Bogart, Humphrey (1899–1957), American film star, renowned for "tough guy" roles as in *The African Queen* (1951).

Bohr, Niels (1885–1962), Danish scientist who organised the first "Atoms for Peace" conference in 1955.

Britten, Benjamin (1913–76), British composer, famed for operas like *Billy Budd* (1951) and *Gloriana* (1953).

Burgess, Guy (1911–63), British diplomat who, with Donald Maclean (1913–), revealed himself as a double agent by defecting to the Soviet Union in 1951. He lived out the rest of his life in exile.

Chaplin, Charlie (1889–1977), British film actor who left the United States for Swiss exile during the McCarthy era. He wrote, directed and starred in the film *Limelight* (1953), the masterpiece of his later career. He also composed its hit theme tune.

De Valera, Eamon (1882–1975), veteran Irish nationalist leader, who served as Prime Minister of the Republic of Ireland 1951–4 and 1957–9 and as its President 1959–73.

Dulles, John Foster (1888–1959), American Secretary of State (1953–9) noted for his unyielding anti-communism and willingness to play at "brinkmanship" in international confrontations.

Einstein, Albert (1879–1955), German-born American scientist whose work in theoretical physics won him the Nobel Prize and made possible the development of atomic weapons. He was himself a passionate supporter of nuclear disarmament and said of his own achievements "If only I had known I should have become a watchmaker".

Gaitskell, Hugh (1906–63), British Labour politician, Chancellor of the Exchequer 1950–1 and Leader of the Opposition (1955–63). Remembered for his efforts to fight the party's support for unilateral nuclear disarmament.

Golding, William (1911–), British author best known for *Lord of the Flies* (1954) which suggested how thin was modern man's veneer of civilisation.

Guinness, Sir Alec (1914–), British film actor, star of *The Bridge on the River Kwai*, knighted in 1959.

Hawthorn, Mike (1929–58), Britain's first motor-racing world champion, killed in a road accident.

Hemingway, Ernest (1899–1961), American adventurer and author of the semi-autobiographical *The Old Man and the Sea* (1952). Winner of the Nobel Prize for Literature 1954.

Kelly Gene (1912–), American singer/dancer/actor best known for *Singin' in the Rain* (1952)

Kelly, Grace (1929–82), American film actress and star of *High Society* (1956) who joined it by marrying Prince Rainier III of Monaco.

Kenyatta, Jomo (1893–1978), African nationalist leader, imprisoned 1953–60 for alleged leadership of the "Mau Mau" rebellion, which he always denied. He became the first Prime Minister of an independent Kenya (1963) and

Charlie Chaplin   Jomo Kenyatta   Nikita Khrushchev

later its president until his death.

Khrushchev, Nikita (1894–1971), First Secretary of the Soviet Communist Party from 1953 and Prime Minister of the Soviet Union 1958–64. He "destalinized" Russia by governing without terror but crushed risings in satellite countries. He improved relations with the West but worsened them with China. Failure of his economic policies drove him from power.

Loewe, Frederick (1901–), American composer of hit musicals *My Fair Lady* (1956) and *Gigi* (1958).

Macmillan, Harold (1894–1986), British Conservative politician who dominated the 1950s as Minister of Housing, Chancellor of the Exchequer and Prime Minister (1957–63). His chief international success was a nuclear "test ban treaty" but he failed to get Britain into the European Economic Community.

Margaret, Princess (1930–), public disapproval in 1955 made it impossible for her to marry divorced Group Captain Peter Townsend. In 1960 she married photographer Anthony Armstrong-Jones.

Menzies, Sir Robert (1894–1978), veteran Australian politician, Prime Minister 1949–66. He favoured close links with the United Kingdom.

Nagy, Imre (1895–1958), lifelong Hungarian communist who, as Prime Minister after the 1956 rising, promised free elections. He was overthrown by Soviet invaders, tried and shot.

Nehru, Jawaharlal (1889–1964), first Prime Minister of independent India (1947–64). He stood for industrial modernization and social reform.

Orwell, George (1903–50), real name Eric Blair, British writer and socialist whose prophetic novel *Nineteen Eighty-four* (1949) warned of the dangers of totalitarian rule.

Pasternak, Boris (1890–1960), Russian poet and author of *Doctor Zhivago*. Winner of the Nobel Prize for Literature in 1958, which he was not allowed to collect as his writing was considered too critical of the Soviet state.

Pearson, Lester (1897–1972), Canadian diplomat, who served as President of the UN General Assembly (1952–3) and won the Nobel Peace Prize in 1957.

Presley, Elvis Aaron (1935–77), American singer and actor. Accused by critics of "sneering with his legs", he won the nickname "Elvis the Pelvis", before outstripping all rivals to become "the King". Served as a private in the US army in Germany

1958–9.

Schweitzer, Albert (1875–1965), medical missionary and talented organist whose work among African lepers won him the Nobel Peace Prize in 1952.

Thomas, Dylan (1914–53), Welsh poet chiefly remembered for his radio verse drama *Under Milk Wood*, read by rising young actor Richard Burton in a posthumous production in 1954.

Harold MacMillan

Elvis Presley

Albert Schweitzer

1950s year by year

1950

- Alger Hiss jailed in America for perjury in concealing Communist party membership.
- Senator McCarthy alleges State Department employs over 200 Communists.
- Fuchs imprisoned for betraying British atom secrets to the Soviet Union.
- Russia announces it has an atom bomb.
- End of petrol rationing in Britain.
- Outbreak of war in Korea leads to involvement of UN and Chinese forces.
- Uruguay win the World Cup.
- Diners Club issues first credit cards.
- Death of George Bernard Shaw.
- General Certificate of Education 'O' and 'A' level examinations introduced.
- Peak District designated as Britain's first National Park.

1951

- President Truman dismisses General MacArthur as Far East commander.
- Festival of Britain.
- Prime Minister Mossadeq nationalises the oil industry in Iran.
- British spies Burgess and Maclean defect to the Soviet Union.
- Conservative government replaces Labour in Britain.
- Libya becomes an independent state.
- *The Archers*, Britain's longest running radio serial begins.
- First Miss World contest staged.
- J. D. Salinger publishes cult novel *The Catcher in the Rye*.
- Death of William Randolph Hearst, eccentric American newspaper tycoon.
- First commercial manufacture of electronic computers.

1952

- Death of King George VI, succession of Queen Elizabeth II.
- Eisenhower wins landslide victory in US Presidential election.
- European Coal and Steel Community established.
- Identity cards abolished in Britain.
- Army coup in Egypt overthrows King Farouk.
- Britain tests atomic bomb.
- 'Mau Mau' movement leads to state of emergency in Kenya.
- Death of Eva Peron, wife of dictator of Argentina.
- United States explodes an H-bomb.
- World's first jet airline service (London-Johannesberg).
- 'Cinerama' wide-screen films first exhibited.
- First transistorised hearing aid.
- First teabags marketed in Britain.
- Agatha Christie's mystery play *The Mousetrap* begins non-stop run.
- Olympic Games held in Helsinki.

1953

- Death of Stalin
- Coronation of Queen Elizabeth II.
- 280 drowned by freak floods along Britain's east coast.
- Hillary and Tenzing conquer Everest.
- Soviet troops crush workers' rising in East Berlin.
- Armistice ends fighting in Korea.
- Military coup in Iran overthrows Mossadeq and reinstates the Shah.
- John F. Kennedy marries Jacqueline Bouvier.
- Winston Churchill wins Nobel Prize for Literature.
- Russians explode an H-bomb in Siberia.
- Ian Fleming publishes first James Bond book *Casino Royale*.
- Samaritans organisation established in London.
- First music synthesizer.

- First car with fibreglass body – the Chevrolet Corvette.

1954

- French army defeated at Dien Bien Phu by Vietnamese.
- Billy Graham crusades in America and Britain.
- Medical research confirms link between smoking and cancer.
- Fall of Senator McCarthy after condemnation by US Senate.
- Food rationing ends in Britain.
- British government orders grounding of all Comets, the world's first jet airliner, after a third mystery crash.
- Japanese crew of fishing boat *Lucky Dragon* contaminated by radioactive fall-out from US H-bomb test at Bikini Atoll.
- Nasser emerges as Egypt's leader.
- Pope launches Eurovision TV network.
- West Germany wins soccer World Cup.
- Roger Bannister runs world's first sub four minute mile.
- Algerian nationalists begin rising against French rule.
- J. R. R. Tolkien publishes *Lord of the Rings*.
- *Nautilus* launched as world's first nuclear submarine.
- Value Added Tax (VAT) introduced in France.

1955

- Churchill replaced by Eden as Prime Minister.
- Warsaw Pact established as Russian-led military alliance.
- Argentine dictator Peron overthrown.
- Gaitskell succeeds Attlee as leader of Labour Party.
- Ruth Ellis hanged for murder, the last woman to be hanged in Britain.
- European Parliament holds first

meeting at Strasbourg.
- Commercial television (ITV) begins in Britain.
- Bus boycott by blacks begins in segregated Montgomery, Alabama.
- Wave of 'Flying Saucer' sightings reported.
- First Wimpy Bar hamburger house opened in London.
- Fibre optics developed at Imperial College, London.
- High-speed dental drill introduced in Sweden.

1956

- Khrushchev denounces Stalin's terror.
- "Premium Bond" savings certificates introduced in Britain.
- Anti-Soviet risings in Poland and Hungary crushed.
- Nasser nationalizes Suez Canal – Britain and France withdraw from abortive invasion of Egypt after disapproval of the United States but Israelis seize Sinai.
- Re-election of Eisenhower as US President.
- Transatlantic telephone service begins.
- Fairey Delta fighter sets air speed record of 1132 mph.
- First video recorder manufactured.
- First Eurovision Song Contest.
- Real Madrid win first European Cup football competition.
- First Go-Kart built.

1957

- Macmillan succeeds Eden as Prime Minister.
- Death of Arturo Toscanini, Italian conductor, aged 89.
- Treaty of Rome establishes European Economic Community.
- Republic of Ireland declares state of emergency to fight the IRA.
- Malaya becomes independent.
- Russia launches *Sputnik I*, the world's first space satellite.
- Death of French designer Christian Dior.
- Gold Coast becomes independent as Ghana.
- Britain tests its own H-bomb.
- Building of Brazil's new capital at Brasilia begins.
- Jodrell Bank radio telescope completed.
- Sony market first pocket-sized transistor radio.
- Soviet Union launches first Intercontinental Ballistic Missile.
- Queen Elizabeth II makes first royal TV Christmas broadcast.
- Frisbee invented in America.

1958

- Munich air crash devastates Manchester United football team.
- Campaign for Nuclear Disarmament (CND) launched in Britain.
- De Gaulle returns to power in France to deal with crisis in Algeria.
- Brazil win soccer world cup.
- Chinese crush national rising in Tibet.
- Surrey win county cricket championship for the seventh year running.
- Race Riots in Notting Hill Gate, London.
- John XXIII becomes Pope.
- Preston by-pass, Britain's first motorway opened.
- "Planetarium" astronomical exhibition opened at Madame Tussaud's, London.
- US forces land in "peace-keeping" operation in Lebanon.
- First stereo records marketed.
- Britain introduces parking meters.
- Moulton small wheel bicycle invented.
- Integrated circuit (microchip) invented.

1959

- Fidel Castro seizes power in Cuba.
- De Gaulle becomes President of the Fifth French Republic.
- Death of American architect Frank Lloyd Wright.
- NASA picks first astronaut squad.
- Schools desegregated by Federal troops in Little Rock, Arkansas.
- Harold Macmillan leads Conservatives to third successive election victory.
- Soviet satellite *Lunik III* sends back first photographs of the far side of the moon.
- European Free Trade Association (EFTA) set up by UK, Austria, Portugal, Switzerland, Sweden, Norway and Denmark.
- Archbishop Makarios becomes first President of the independent Republic of Cyprus.
- Alaska becomes 49th state of the United States.
- Singapore becomes independent.
- Hawaii becomes 50th state of the United States.
- Hovercraft makes maiden cross-Channel voyage.
- First section of M1 Motorway opened in Britain.
- First identikit pictures used for criminal identification.
- First transatlantic TV transmission.
- First charity walk.

Index